THIS PLANNER BELONGS TO:

- **NAME**
- **ICE RINK | CLUB**
- **COACH**
- **IF FOUND, PLEASE RETURN TO**
- **MOBILE**
- **EMAIL**

IN CASE OF EMERGENCY, PLEASE CONTACT:

- **NAME**
- **RELATIONSHIP**
- **PHONE**
- **EMAIL**

- **NAME**
- **RELATIONSHIP**
- **PHONE**
- **EMAIL**

Copyright © 2021 by Aimée Ricca
All Rights Reserved.

This publication is copyrighted and is solely for *your* personal use.

No part of this book may be reproduced in any form or by any electronic means including information storage and retrieval systems—except in the case of brief quotations embodied in critical articles or reviews—without express permission from its publisher. Aimée Ricca.

This publication is designed to provide accurate and authoritative informationin regard to the subject matter covered. It is sold with the understanding that the publisher is not engaged in rendering legal, accounting, or other professional services. If legal or other expert advice is required, the services of a competent professional person should be sought.—*From a Declaration of Principals Jointly Adopted by a Committee of the American Bar and a Committee of Publishers and Associations*

All brand names and product names used in this book are trademarks, registered trademarks, or trade names of their respective holders. Aimée Ricca is not associated with any product or vendor in this book.

The information contained herein is provided for educational purposes only and is not intended to substitute for the advice of a health care provider. Before starting any exercise or nutrition program, consult a physician.

ISBN: 9798522444716

Library of Congress Cataloging-in-Publication Data:

Names: Ricca, Aimee, author.
Title: Annual figure skating planner : every skater needs a plan / Aimee Ricca.
Description: Parsippany : Aimee Ricca, 2021
Identifiers: LCCN PENDING (print)
Subjects: LCSH
Classification: LCC PENDING

skatewithaimee.com | aimeericca.com | hello@aimeericca.com

FREE STUFF

If you enjoy getting stuff for free, sign-up for my mailing list!

Just Go To:

www.skatewithaimee.com/freebies

WELCOME!

Planning helps you to focus your energy in a productive way that can help you make measurable progress in your skating and other areas of your life.

I've created this planner for you to help you with your planning, provide direction, as well as keep you moving forward and motivated for the entire year!

Bring this planner with you to all your lessons, practices, and training sessions, so that you and your coach can take notes and track your progress throughout the year.

You will find the planner is especially useful when you are practicing on your own to keep you focused so that you can work on the elements that will help you to reach your goals.

Wishing you an amazing year of success!

Aimée

Aimée Ricca
PSA Ranked & Rated Figure Skating Coach | Choreographer
ISSA Certified ISSA Elite Trainer (E-CPT),
Strength & Conditioning Specialist (CSSC),
Nutritionist Coach (CN, Pn1), Youth Sports Coach (CYFC, YFS-1, YNS)
NSCA Member & Participant in Figure Skating Special Interest Group

GETTING STARTED!

This planner is your personal roadmap to success!

The first section of this planner contains pages for you to journal, set goals, and create your personal training plan.

Use these pages to reflect on your skating, set new goals with your coach, and map out your annual training plan.

The next section of this planner is for you to create a plan for every practice and training section - on and off the ice.

Use these pages to make the most of your ice and workout sessions so that you never have to figure out what you should be working on!

The final section of this planner is for you to track your progress.

Use these pages to measure your progress. I suggest that you review and evaluate your program every three months and make adjustments so that you can continue to improve.

MY LIFE ON ICE

Insert your favorite picture of you skating, or draw yourself skating here:

I spent ____ hours training on ice each week. I spent ___ hours training off-ice each week.

My lesson, ice session, and off-ice training session days and times:

My skating friends:

The skater that I most admire is:_____.

I admire them because:

MY LIFE ON ICE

I skate because:	When I skate, I feel:

I am most inspired by:	I will have achieved my skating dreams when:

MY SKATING SKILLS

Discuss with your coach and list the skills that you have mastered (can perform correctly 8 out of 10 times), and the skills you are developing:

SKILLS I HAVE MASTERED:

SKILLS I AM WORKING TO MASTER:

SETTING GOALS

Evaluate Your Previous Year

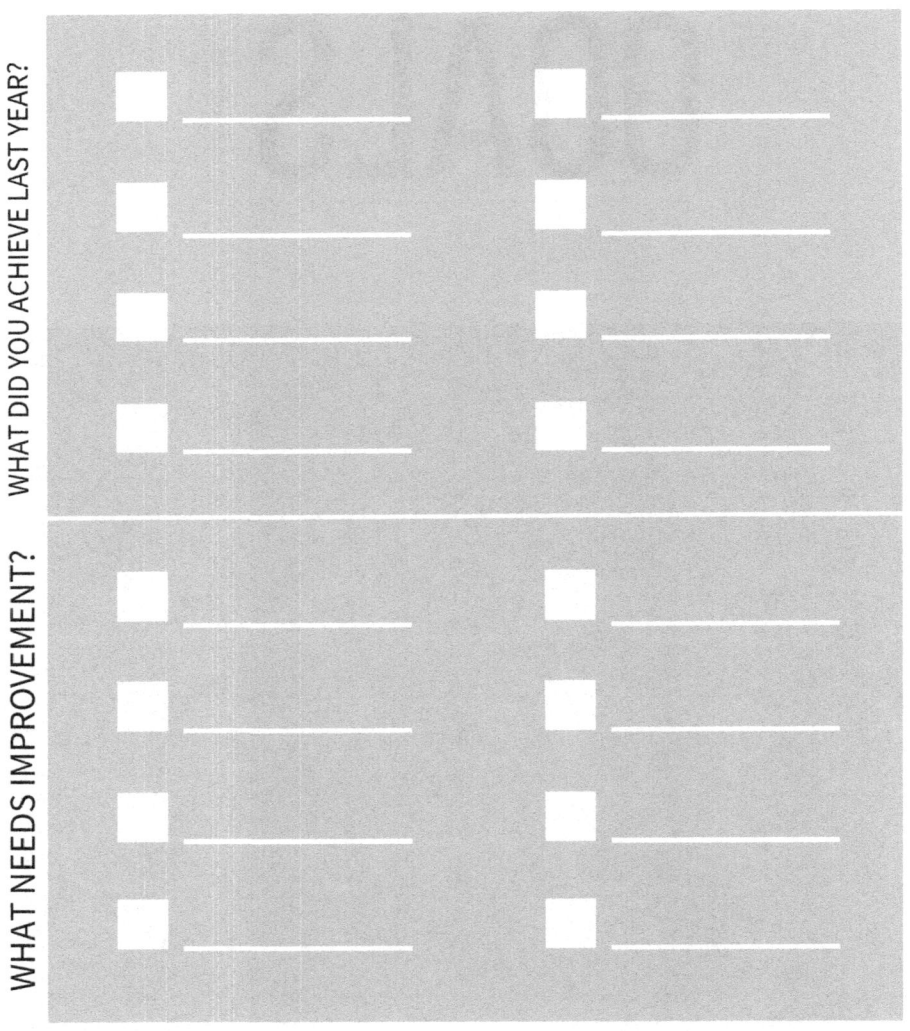

LOOK AHEAD

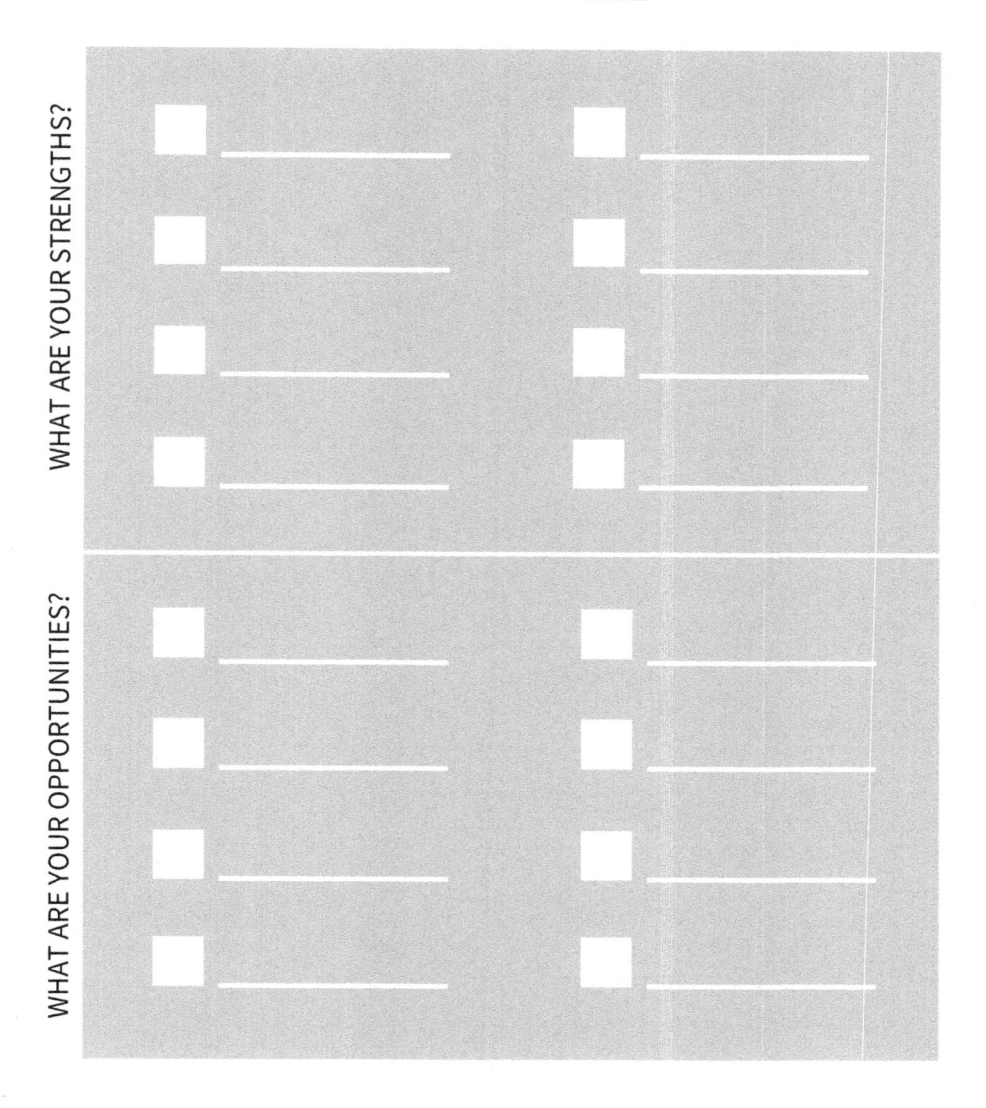

WHAT ARE YOUR STRENGTHS?

- _____
- _____
- _____
- _____

- _____
- _____
- _____
- _____

WHAT ARE YOUR OPPORTUNITIES?

- _____
- _____
- _____
- _____

- _____
- _____
- _____
- _____

THOUGHTS...

SKATER

COACH

CREATE YOUR VISION!

Take some time and reflect over the past year.

Think about the year and ask yourself the following questions...

What experiences made you feel happy?

What experiences changed you?

What held you back?

What have you achieved in different parts of your life?

How is your health, fitness, and wellness?

How did you build relationships with friends & family?

VISION & MISSION

Now, envision your next year. For each of the boxes below think about how you envision each of the aspects listed.

Think about the WHY behind what you write down.

Notice if there are words or mantras that jump out at you for this next year.

SCHOOL & EDUCATION	FITNESS & HEALTH

RELATIONSHIPS	SKATING & SPORTS

EXPERIENCES	MINDSET

SET YEARLY GOALS

First think about the big picture of what you really want to achieve. Think of goals that can be measured and will keep you motivated and inspired throughout the year.

	THINGS TO WORK ON	HOW CAN YOU MEASURE?	BY WHEN?
SKATING ELEMENTS			
MOVES IN THE FIELD			
DANCE / FS TESTS			
SKATING COMPETITIONS			

SET YEARLY GOALS

First think about the big picture of what you really want to achieve. Think of goals that can be measured and will keep you motivated and inspired throughout the year.

	THINGS TO WORK ON	HOW CAN YOU MEASURE?	BY WHEN?
MINDSET SKILLS			
OFF-ICE TRAINING			
SCHOOL & EDUCATION			
FAMILY & FRIENDS			

SET YEARLY GOALS

First think about the big picture of what you really want to achieve. Think of goals that can be measured and will keep you motivated and inspired throughout the year.

	THINGS TO WORK ON	HOW CAN YOU MEASURE?	BY WHEN?
EXPERIENCES			
OTHER			
OTHER			
OTHER			

MILESTONES

Now pick three goals and break each one down
into measurable ways to achieve it!

GOAL #1:

Write down 10 measurable ways to achieve your goal.

1.
2.
3.
4.
5.
6.
7.
8.
9.
10.

Choose 3 from your list above to focus on.
These will be your major milestones, or short-term goals.

1.
2.
3.

MILESTONES

Now pick three goals and break each one down
into measurable ways to achieve it!

GOAL #2:

Write down 10 measurable ways to achieve your goal.

1.
2.
3.
4.
5.
6.
7.
8.
9.
10.

Choose 3 from your list above to focus on.
These will be your major milestones, or short-term goals.

1.
2.
3.

MILESTONES

Now pick three goals and break each one down
into measurable ways to achieve it!

GOAL #3:

Write down 10 measurable ways to achieve your goal.

1.
2.
3.
4.
5.
6.
7.
8.
9.
10.

Choose 3 from your list above to focus on.
These will be your major milestones, or short-term goals.

1.
2.
3.

GOALS

Now, use this page to place your goals in the first column.
Then, list your milestones (short-term goals) in the second column with the due date.
As you complete your milestones, use the checkmark column to mark them completed!

GOAL	HOW WILL YOU GET THERE?	DEADLINE	✓
	....		
	....		
	....		
	....		
	....		
	....		

GOAL	HOW WILL YOU GET THERE?	DEADLINE	✓
	....		
	....		
	....		
	....		
	....		
	....		

GOAL	HOW WILL YOU GET THERE?	DEADLINE	✓
	....		
	....		
	....		
	....		
	....		
	....		

KEY EVENTS

Map out any key dates such as competitions, tests, clinics, and other special events.

JANUARY	FEBRUARY	MARCH

APRIL	MAY	JUNE

JULY	AUGUST	SEPTEMBER

OCTOBER	NOVEMBER	DECEMBER

ROAD MAP

Map out your milestones for each month below:

JANUARY	FEBRUARY	MARCH

APRIL	MAY	JUNE

JULY	AUGUST	SEPTEMBER

OCTOBER	NOVEMBER	DECEMBER

MY NOTES

COACH'S NOTES

TAKE ACTION!

MY WEEK

DATE:

PRIORITIES:

TO DO:

MON

TUE

WED

THU

FRI

SAT

SUN

MY WEEK

DATE:

PRIORITIES:

TO DO:

MON

TUE

WED

THU

FRI

SAT

SUN

MY WEEK

DATE:

PRIORITIES:

TO DO:

MON

TUE

WED

THU

FRI

SAT

SUN

MY WEEK

DATE:

PRIORITIES:

TO DO:

MON

TUE

WED

THU

FRI

SAT

SUN

MY WEEK

DATE:

PRIORITIES:

TO DO:

MON

TUE

WED

THU

FRI

SAT

SUN

MY WEEK

DATE:

PRIORITIES:

TO DO:

MON

TUE

WED

THU

FRI

SAT

SUN

MY WEEK

DATE:

PRIORITIES:

TO DO:

MON

TUE

WED

THU

FRI

SAT

SUN

MY WEEK

DATE:

PRIORITIES:

TO DO:

MON

TUE

WED

THU

FRI

SAT

SUN

MY WEEK

DATE:

PRIORITIES:

TO DO:

MON

TUE

WED

THU

FRI

SAT

SUN

MY WEEK

DATE:

PRIORITIES:

TO DO:

MON

TUE

WED

THU

FRI

SAT

SUN

MY WEEK

DATE:

PRIORITIES:

TO DO:

MON

TUE

WED

THU

FRI

SAT

SUN

MY WEEK

DATE:

PRIORITIES:

TO DO:

MON

TUE

WED

THU

FRI

SAT

SUN

MY WEEK

DATE:

PRIORITIES:

TO DO:

MON

TUE

WED

THU

FRI

SAT

SUN

MY WEEK

DATE:

PRIORITIES:

TO DO:

MON

TUE

WED

THU

FRI

SAT

SUN

MY WEEK

DATE:

PRIORITIES:

TO DO:

MON

TUE

WED

THU

FRI

SAT

SUN

MY WEEK

DATE:

PRIORITIES:

TO DO:

MON

TUE

WED

THU

FRI

SAT

SUN

MY WEEK

DATE:

PRIORITIES:

TO DO:

MON

TUE

WED

THU

FRI

SAT

SUN

MY WEEK

DATE:

PRIORITIES:

TO DO:

MON

TUE

WED

THU

FRI

SAT

SUN

MY WEEK

DATE:

PRIORITIES:

TO DO:

MON

TUE

WED

THU

FRI

SAT

SUN

MY WEEK

DATE:

PRIORITIES:

TO DO:

MON

TUE

WED

THU

FRI

SAT

SUN

MY WEEK

DATE:

PRIORITIES:

TO DO:

MON

TUE

WED

THU

FRI

SAT

SUN

MY WEEK

DATE:

PRIORITIES:

TO DO:

MON

TUE

WED

THU

FRI

SAT

SUN

MY WEEK

DATE:

PRIORITIES:

TO DO:

MON

TUE

WED

THU

FRI

SAT

SUN

MY WEEK

DATE:

PRIORITIES:

TO DO:

MON

TUE

WED

THU

FRI

SAT

SUN

MY WEEK

DATE:

PRIORITIES:

TO DO:

MON

TUE

WED

THU

FRI

SAT

SUN

MY WEEK

DATE:

PRIORITIES:

TO DO:

MON

TUE

WED

THU

FRI

SAT

SUN

MY WEEK

DATE:

PRIORITIES:

TO DO:

MON

TUE

WED

THU

FRI

SAT

SUN

MY WEEK

DATE:

PRIORITIES:

TO DO:

MON

TUE

WED

THU

FRI

SAT

SUN

MY WEEK

DATE:

PRIORITIES:

TO DO:

MON

TUE

WED

THU

FRI

SAT

SUN

MY WEEK

DATE:

PRIORITIES:

TO DO:

MON

TUE

WED

THU

FRI

SAT

SUN

MY WEEK

DATE:

PRIORITIES:

TO DO:

MON

TUE

WED

THU

FRI

SAT

SUN

MY WEEK

DATE:

PRIORITIES:

TO DO:

MON

TUE

WED

THU

FRI

SAT

SUN

MY WEEK

DATE:

PRIORITIES:

TO DO:

MON

TUE

WED

THU

FRI

SAT

SUN

MY WEEK

DATE:

PRIORITIES:

TO DO:

MON

TUE

WED

THU

FRI

SAT

SUN

MY WEEK

DATE:

PRIORITIES:

TO DO:

MON

TUE

WED

THU

FRI

SAT

SUN

MY WEEK

DATE:

PRIORITIES:

TO DO:

MON

TUE

WED

THU

FRI

SAT

SUN

MY WEEK

DATE:

PRIORITIES:

TO DO:

MON

TUE

WED

THU

FRI

SAT

SUN

MY WEEK

DATE:

PRIORITIES:

TO DO:

MON

TUE

WED

THU

FRI

SAT

SUN

MY WEEK

DATE:

PRIORITIES:

TO DO:

MON

TUE

WED

THU

FRI

SAT

SUN

MY WEEK

DATE:

PRIORITIES:

TO DO:

MON

TUE

WED

THU

FRI

SAT

SUN

MY WEEK

DATE:

PRIORITIES:

TO DO:

MON

TUE

WED

THU

FRI

SAT

SUN

MY WEEK

DATE:

PRIORITIES:

TO DO:

MON

TUE

WED

THU

FRI

SAT

SUN

MY WEEK

DATE:

PRIORITIES:

TO DO:

MON

TUE

WED

THU

FRI

SAT

SUN

MY WEEK

DATE:

PRIORITIES:

TO DO:

MON

TUE

WED

THU

FRI

SAT

SUN

MY WEEK

DATE:

PRIORITIES:

TO DO:

MON

TUE

WED

THU

FRI

SAT

SUN

MY WEEK

DATE:

PRIORITIES:

TO DO:

MON

TUE

WED

THU

FRI

SAT

SUN

MY WEEK

DATE:

PRIORITIES:

TO DO:

MON

TUE

WED

THU

FRI

SAT

SUN

MY WEEK

DATE:

PRIORITIES:

TO DO:

MON

TUE

WED

THU

FRI

SAT

SUN

MY WEEK

DATE:

PRIORITIES:

TO DO:

MON

TUE

WED

THU

FRI

SAT

SUN

MY WEEK

DATE:

PRIORITIES:

TO DO:

MON

TUE

WED

THU

FRI

SAT

SUN

MY WEEK

DATE:

PRIORITIES:

TO DO:

MON

TUE

WED

THU

FRI

SAT

SUN

MY WEEK

DATE:

PRIORITIES:

TO DO:

MON

TUE

WED

THU

FRI

SAT

SUN

MY WEEK

DATE:

PRIORITIES:

TO DO:

MON

TUE

WED

THU

FRI

SAT

SUN

MY WEEK

DATE:

PRIORITIES:

TO DO:

MON

TUE

WED

THU

FRI

SAT

SUN

MY OFF-ICE WARM-UP

Work with your off-ice strength and conditioning coach/trainer to come up with your off-ice warm-up routine. Remember to complete it before each of your skating sessions and check-off each as your complete it.

MONTH:

_____
_____
_____
_____
_____
_____
_____
_____
_____
_____

IMPORTANT THINGS TO REMEMBER:

1. ....
2. ....
3. ....

SKATING PRACTICE

Work with your skating coach to come up with your skating practice list. Remember to complete each item on the list during every practice session and check-off each as your complete it.

MONTH:

_____
_____
_____
_____
_____
_____
_____
_____
_____
_____
_____

COACH'S NOTES:

....
....
....
....

MY OFF-ICE COOLDOWN

Work with your off-ice strength and conditioning coach/trainer to come up with your off-ice cooldown/stretch routine.
Remember to complete it after each of your skating sessions and check-off each as your complete it.

MONTH:

_____
_____
_____
_____
_____
_____
_____
_____
_____
_____

IMPORTANT THINGS TO REMEMBER:

1. ....
2. ....
3. ....

MY OFF-ICE TRAINING

Work with your off-ice strength and conditioning coach/trainer to come up with your off-ice workout routine.
Remember to complete it according to the schedule your trainer recommends and check-off each as your complete it.

MONTH:

_____
_____
_____
_____
_____
_____
_____
_____
_____
_____
_____
_____

IMPORTANT THINGS TO REMEMBER:

1. ....
2. ....
3. ....

THOUGHTS...

SKATER

COACH

MY OFF-ICE WARM-UP

Work with your off-ice strength and conditioning coach/trainer to come up with your off-ice warm-up routine. Remember to complete it before each of your skating sessions and check-off each as your complete it.

MONTH:

_____
_____
_____
_____
_____
_____
_____
_____
_____
_____
_____
_____

IMPORTANT THINGS TO REMEMBER:

1. ....
2. ....
3. ....

SKATING PRACTICE

Work with your skating coach to come up with your skating practice list. Remember to complete each item on the list during every practice session and check-off each as your complete it.

MONTH:

_____
_____
_____
_____
_____
_____
_____
_____
_____
_____

COACH'S NOTES:

....
....
....
....

MY OFF-ICE COOLDOWN

Work with your off-ice strength and conditioning coach/trainer to come up with your off-ice cooldown/stretch routine.
Remember to complete it after each of your skating sessions and check-off each as your complete it.

MONTH:

_____
_____
_____
_____
_____
_____
_____
_____
_____
_____
_____

IMPORTANT THINGS TO REMEMBER:

1. ....
2. ....
3. ....

MY OFF-ICE TRAINING

Work with your off-ice strength and conditioning coach/trainer to come up with your off-ice workout routine.
Remember to complete it according to the schedule your trainer recommends and check-off each as your complete it.

MONTH:

IMPORTANT THINGS TO REMEMBER:

1. ....
2. ....
3. ....

THOUGHTS...

SKATER

COACH

MY OFF-ICE WARM-UP

Work with your off-ice strength and conditioning coach/trainer to come up with your off-ice warm-up routine. Remember to complete it before each of your skating sessions and check-off each as your complete it.

MONTH:

_____
_____
_____
_____
_____
_____
_____
_____
_____
_____

IMPORTANT THINGS TO REMEMBER:

1. ....
2. ....
3. ....

SKATING PRACTICE

Work with your skating coach to come up with your skating practice list. Remember to complete each item on the list during every practice session and check-off each as your complete it.

MONTH:

COACH'S NOTES:

MY OFF-ICE COOLDOWN

Work with your off-ice strength and conditioning coach/trainer to come up with your off-ice cooldown/stretch routine.
Remember to complete it after each of your skating sessions and check-off each as your complete it.

MONTH:

_____
_____
_____
_____
_____
_____
_____
_____
_____
_____

IMPORTANT THINGS TO REMEMBER:

1. ....
2. ....
3. ....

MY OFF-ICE TRAINING

Work with your off-ice strength and conditioning coach/trainer to come up with your off-ice workout routine.
Remember to complete it according to the schedule your trainer recommends and check-off each as your complete it.

MONTH:

_____
_____
_____
_____
_____
_____
_____
_____
_____
_____

IMPORTANT THINGS TO REMEMBER:

1. ....
2. ....
3. ....

THOUGHTS...

SKATER

COACH

MY OFF-ICE WARM-UP

Work with your off-ice strength and conditioning coach/trainer to come up with your off-ice warm-up routine. Remember to complete it before each of your skating sessions and check-off each as your complete it.

MONTH:

_____

_____

_____

_____

_____

_____

_____

_____

_____

_____

_____

IMPORTANT THINGS TO REMEMBER:

1. ....

2. ....

3. ....

SKATING PRACTICE

Work with your skating coach to come up with your skating practice list. Remember to complete each item on the list during every practice session and check-off each as your complete it.

MONTH:

_____
_____
_____
_____
_____
_____
_____
_____
_____
_____

COACH'S NOTES:

....
....
....
....

MY OFF-ICE COOLDOWN

Work with your off-ice strength and conditioning coach/trainer to come up with your off-ice cooldown/stretch routine.
Remember to complete it after each of your skating sessions and check-off each as your complete it.

MONTH:

_____
_____
_____
_____
_____
_____
_____
_____
_____
_____
_____
_____

IMPORTANT THINGS TO REMEMBER:

1. ....
2. ....
3. ....

MY OFF-ICE TRAINING

Work with your off-ice strength and conditioning coach/trainer to come up with your off-ice workout routine.
Remember to complete it according to the schedule your trainer recommends and check-off each as your complete it.

MONTH:

IMPORTANT THINGS TO REMEMBER:

1. ....
2. ....
3. ....

THOUGHTS...

SKATER

COACH

MY OFF-ICE WARM-UP

Work with your off-ice strength and conditioning coach/trainer to come up with your off-ice warm-up routine. Remember to complete it before each of your skating sessions and check-off each as your complete it.

MONTH:

_____
_____
_____
_____
_____
_____
_____
_____
_____
_____

IMPORTANT THINGS TO REMEMBER:

1. ....
2. ....
3. ....

SKATING PRACTICE

Work with your skating coach to come up with your skating practice list. Remember to complete each item on the list during every practice session and check-off each as your complete it.

MONTH:

_____
_____
_____
_____
_____
_____
_____
_____
_____
_____
_____
_____

COACH'S NOTES:

....
....
....
....

MY OFF-ICE COOLDOWN

Work with your off-ice strength and conditioning coach/trainer to come up with your off-ice cooldown/stretch routine.
Remember to complete it after each of your skating sessions and check-off each as your complete it.

MONTH:

IMPORTANT THINGS TO REMEMBER:

1. ....
2. ....
3. ....

MY OFF-ICE TRAINING

Work with your off-ice strength and conditioning coach/trainer to come up with your off-ice workout routine.
Remember to complete it according to the schedule your trainer recommends and check-off each as your complete it.

MONTH:

_____
_____
_____
_____
_____
_____
_____
_____
_____
_____
_____

IMPORTANT THINGS TO REMEMBER:

1. ....
2. ....
3. ....

THOUGHTS...

SKATER

COACH

MY OFF-ICE WARM-UP

Work with your off-ice strength and conditioning coach/trainer to come up with your off-ice warm-up routine. Remember to complete it before each of your skating sessions and check-off each as your complete it.

MONTH:

_____
_____
_____
_____
_____
_____
_____
_____
_____
_____

IMPORTANT THINGS TO REMEMBER:

1. ....
2. ....
3. ....

SKATING PRACTICE

Work with your skating coach to come up with your skating practice list. Remember to complete each item on the list during every practice session and check-off each as your complete it.

MONTH:

_____
_____
_____
_____
_____
_____
_____
_____
_____
_____
_____
_____

COACH'S NOTES:

....
....
....
....

MY OFF-ICE COOLDOWN

Work with your off-ice strength and conditioning coach/trainer to come up with your off-ice cooldown/stretch routine.
Remember to complete it after each of your skating sessions and check-off each as your complete it.

MONTH:

_____

_____

_____

_____

_____

_____

_____

_____

_____

_____

IMPORTANT THINGS TO REMEMBER:

1. ....

2. ....

3. ....

MY OFF-ICE TRAINING

Work with your off-ice strength and conditioning coach/trainer to come up with your off-ice workout routine.
Remember to complete it according to the schedule your trainer recommends and check-off each as your complete it.

MONTH:

_____
_____
_____
_____
_____
_____
_____
_____
_____
_____

IMPORTANT THINGS TO REMEMBER:

1. ....
2. ....
3. ....

THOUGHTS...

SKATER

COACH

MY OFF-ICE WARM-UP

Work with your off-ice strength and conditioning coach/trainer to come up with your off-ice warm-up routine. Remember to complete it before each of your skating sessions and check-off each as your complete it.

MONTH:

_____
_____
_____
_____
_____
_____
_____
_____
_____
_____
_____

IMPORTANT THINGS TO REMEMBER:

1. ....
2. ....
3. ....

SKATING PRACTICE

Work with your skating coach to come up with your skating practice list. Remember to complete each item on the list during every practice session and check-off each as your complete it.

MONTH:

COACH'S NOTES:

....
....
....
....

MY OFF-ICE COOLDOWN

Work with your off-ice strength and conditioning coach/trainer to come up with your off-ice cooldown/stretch routine.
Remember to complete it after each of your skating sessions and check-off each as your complete it.

MONTH:

_____
_____
_____
_____
_____
_____
_____
_____
_____
_____

IMPORTANT THINGS TO REMEMBER:

1. ....
2. ....
3. ....

MY OFF-ICE TRAINING

Work with your off-ice strength and conditioning coach/trainer to come up with your off-ice workout routine.
Remember to complete it according to the schedule your trainer recommends and check-off each as your complete it.

MONTH:

_____
_____
_____
_____
_____
_____
_____
_____
_____
_____
_____
_____

IMPORTANT THINGS TO REMEMBER:

1. ....
2. ....
3. ....

THOUGHTS...

SKATER

COACH

MY OFF-ICE WARM-UP

Work with your off-ice strength and conditioning coach/trainer to come up with your off-ice warm-up routine. Remember to complete it before each of your skating sessions and check-off each as your complete it.

MONTH:

_____
_____
_____
_____
_____
_____
_____
_____
_____
_____
_____
_____

IMPORTANT THINGS TO REMEMBER:

1. ....
2. ....
3. ....

SKATING PRACTICE

Work with your skating coach to come up with your skating practice list. Remember to complete each item on the list during every practice session and check-off each as your complete it.

MONTH:

_____
_____
_____
_____
_____
_____
_____
_____
_____
_____

COACH'S NOTES:

....
....
....
....

MY OFF-ICE COOLDOWN

Work with your off-ice strength and conditioning coach/trainer to come up with your off-ice cooldown/stretch routine.
Remember to complete it after each of your skating sessions and check-off each as your complete it.

MONTH:

_____
_____
_____
_____
_____
_____
_____
_____
_____
_____
_____

IMPORTANT THINGS TO REMEMBER:

1. ....
2. ....
3. ....

MY OFF-ICE TRAINING

Work with your off-ice strength and conditioning coach/trainer to come up with your off-ice workout routine.
Remember to complete it according to the schedule your trainer recommends and check-off each as your complete it.

MONTH:

_____
_____
_____
_____
_____
_____
_____
_____
_____
_____
_____
_____

IMPORTANT THINGS TO REMEMBER:

1. ....
2. ....
3. ....

THOUGHTS...

SKATER

COACH

MY OFF-ICE WARM-UP

Work with your off-ice strength and conditioning coach/trainer to come up with your off-ice warm-up routine. Remember to complete it before each of your skating sessions and check-off each as your complete it.

MONTH:

_____
_____
_____
_____
_____
_____
_____
_____
_____
_____

IMPORTANT THINGS TO REMEMBER:

1. ....
2. ....
3. ....

SKATING PRACTICE

Work with your skating coach to come up with your skating practice list. Remember to complete each item on the list during every practice session and check-off each as your complete it.

MONTH:

_____
_____
_____
_____
_____
_____
_____
_____
_____
_____
_____

COACH'S NOTES:

....
....
....
....

MY OFF-ICE COOLDOWN

Work with your off-ice strength and conditioning coach/trainer to come up with your off-ice cooldown/stretch routine.
Remember to complete it after each of your skating sessions and check-off each as your complete it.

MONTH:

_____
_____
_____
_____
_____
_____
_____
_____
_____
_____
_____
_____

IMPORTANT THINGS TO REMEMBER:

1. ....
2. ....
3. ....

MY OFF-ICE TRAINING

Work with your off-ice strength and conditioning coach/trainer to come up with your off-ice workout routine.
Remember to complete it according to the schedule your trainer recommends and check-off each as your complete it.

MONTH:

_____
_____
_____
_____
_____
_____
_____
_____
_____
_____
_____

IMPORTANT THINGS TO REMEMBER:

1. ....
2. ....
3. ....

THOUGHTS...

SKATER

COACH

MY OFF-ICE WARM-UP

Work with your off-ice strength and conditioning coach/trainer to come up with your off-ice warm-up routine. Remember to complete it before each of your skating sessions and check-off each as your complete it.

MONTH:

_____
_____
_____
_____
_____
_____
_____
_____
_____
_____
_____
_____

IMPORTANT THINGS TO REMEMBER:

1. ....
2. ....
3. ....

SKATING PRACTICE

Work with your skating coach to come up with your skating practice list. Remember to complete each item on the list during every practice session and check-off each as your complete it.

MONTH:

_____
_____
_____
_____
_____
_____
_____
_____
_____
_____
_____
_____

COACH'S NOTES:

....
....
....
....

MY OFF-ICE COOLDOWN

Work with your off-ice strength and conditioning coach/trainer to come up with your off-ice cooldown/stretch routine.
Remember to complete it after each of your skating sessions and check-off each as your complete it.

MONTH:

_____
_____
_____
_____
_____
_____
_____
_____
_____
_____

IMPORTANT THINGS TO REMEMBER:

1. ....
2. ....
3. ....

MY OFF-ICE TRAINING

Work with your off-ice strength and conditioning coach/trainer to come up with your off-ice workout routine.
Remember to complete it according to the schedule your trainer recommends and check-off each as your complete it.

MONTH:

_____
_____
_____
_____
_____
_____
_____
_____
_____
_____
_____

IMPORTANT THINGS TO REMEMBER:

1. ....

2. ....

3. ....

THOUGHTS...

SKATER

COACH

MY OFF-ICE WARM-UP

Work with your off-ice strength and conditioning coach/trainer to come up with your off-ice warm-up routine. Remember to complete it before each of your skating sessions and check-off each as your complete it.

MONTH:

IMPORTANT THINGS TO REMEMBER:

1. ....
2. ....
3. ....

SKATING PRACTICE

Work with your skating coach to come up with your skating practice list. Remember to complete each item on the list during every practice session and check-off each as your complete it.

MONTH:

_____
_____
_____
_____
_____
_____
_____
_____
_____
_____
_____
_____

COACH'S NOTES:

....
....
....
....

MY OFF-ICE COOLDOWN

Work with your off-ice strength and conditioning coach/trainer to come up with your off-ice cooldown/stretch routine.
Remember to complete it after each of your skating sessions and check-off each as your complete it.

MONTH:

_____
_____
_____
_____
_____
_____
_____
_____
_____
_____
_____
_____

IMPORTANT THINGS TO REMEMBER:

1. ....
2. ....
3. ....

MY OFF-ICE TRAINING

Work with your off-ice strength and conditioning coach/trainer to come up with your off-ice workout routine.
Remember to complete it according to the schedule your trainer recommends and check-off each as your complete it.

MONTH:

_____
_____
_____
_____
_____
_____
_____
_____
_____
_____

IMPORTANT THINGS TO REMEMBER:

1. ....
2. ....
3. ....

THOUGHTS...

SKATER

COACH

MY OFF-ICE WARM-UP

Work with your off-ice strength and conditioning coach/trainer to come up with your off-ice warm-up routine. Remember to complete it before each of your skating sessions and check-off each as your complete it.

MONTH:

_____
_____
_____
_____
_____
_____
_____
_____
_____
_____
_____
_____

IMPORTANT THINGS TO REMEMBER:

1. ....
2. ....
3. ....

SKATING PRACTICE

Work with your skating coach to come up with your skating practice list. Remember to complete each item on the list during every practice session and check-off each as your complete it.

MONTH:

COACH'S NOTES:

MY OFF-ICE COOLDOWN

Work with your off-ice strength and conditioning coach/trainer to come up with your off-ice cooldown/stretch routine.
Remember to complete it after each of your skating sessions and check-off each as your complete it.

MONTH:

_____
_____
_____
_____
_____
_____
_____
_____
_____
_____

IMPORTANT THINGS TO REMEMBER:

1. ....
2. ....
3. ....

MY OFF-ICE TRAINING

Work with your off-ice strength and conditioning coach/trainer to come up with your off-ice workout routine.
Remember to complete it according to the schedule your trainer recommends and check-off each as your complete it.

MONTH:

_____
_____
_____
_____
_____
_____
_____
_____
_____
_____
_____

IMPORTANT THINGS TO REMEMBER:

1. ....
2. ....
3. ....

THOUGHTS...

SKATER

COACH

MY PROGRAM ELEMENTS

PROGRAM_____

MUSIC_____

NOTES

PROGRAM COREOGRAPHY

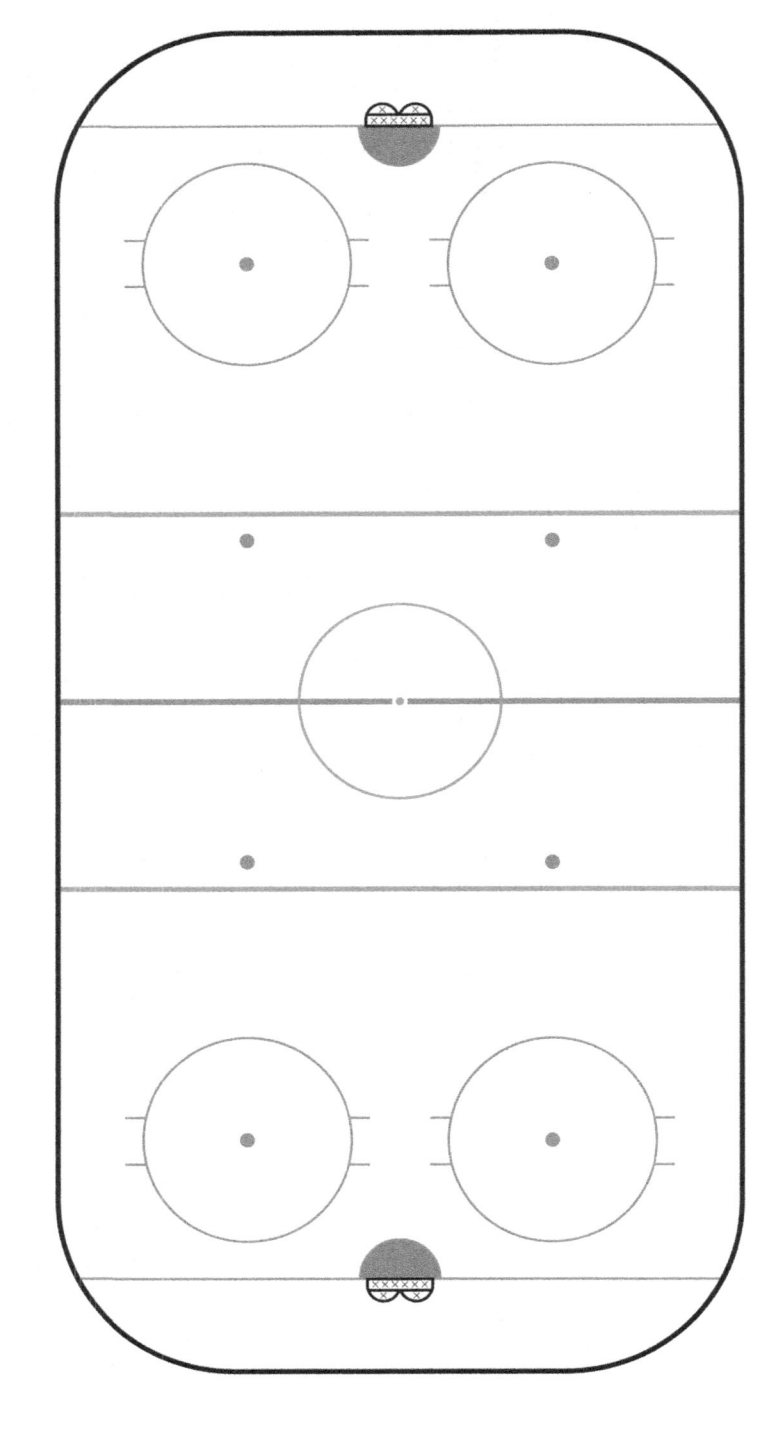

MUSIC: _____

PROGRAM: _____

MY PROGRAM ELEMENTS

PROGRAM_____

MUSIC_____

NOTES

PROGRAM COREOGRAPHY

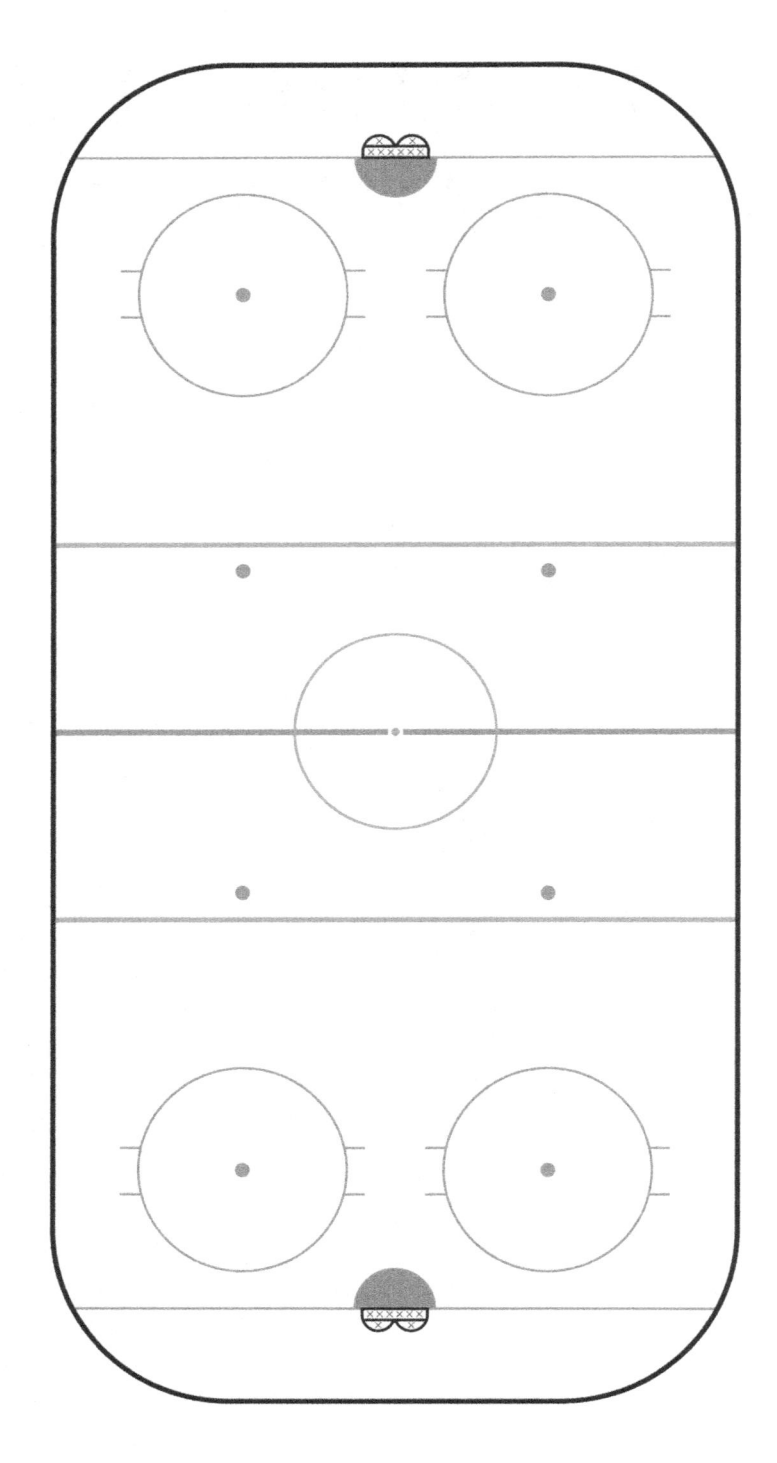

MUSIC: _____

PROGRAM: _____

MY PROGRAM ELEMENTS

PROGRAM_____

MUSIC_____

NOTES

PROGRAM COREOGRAPHY

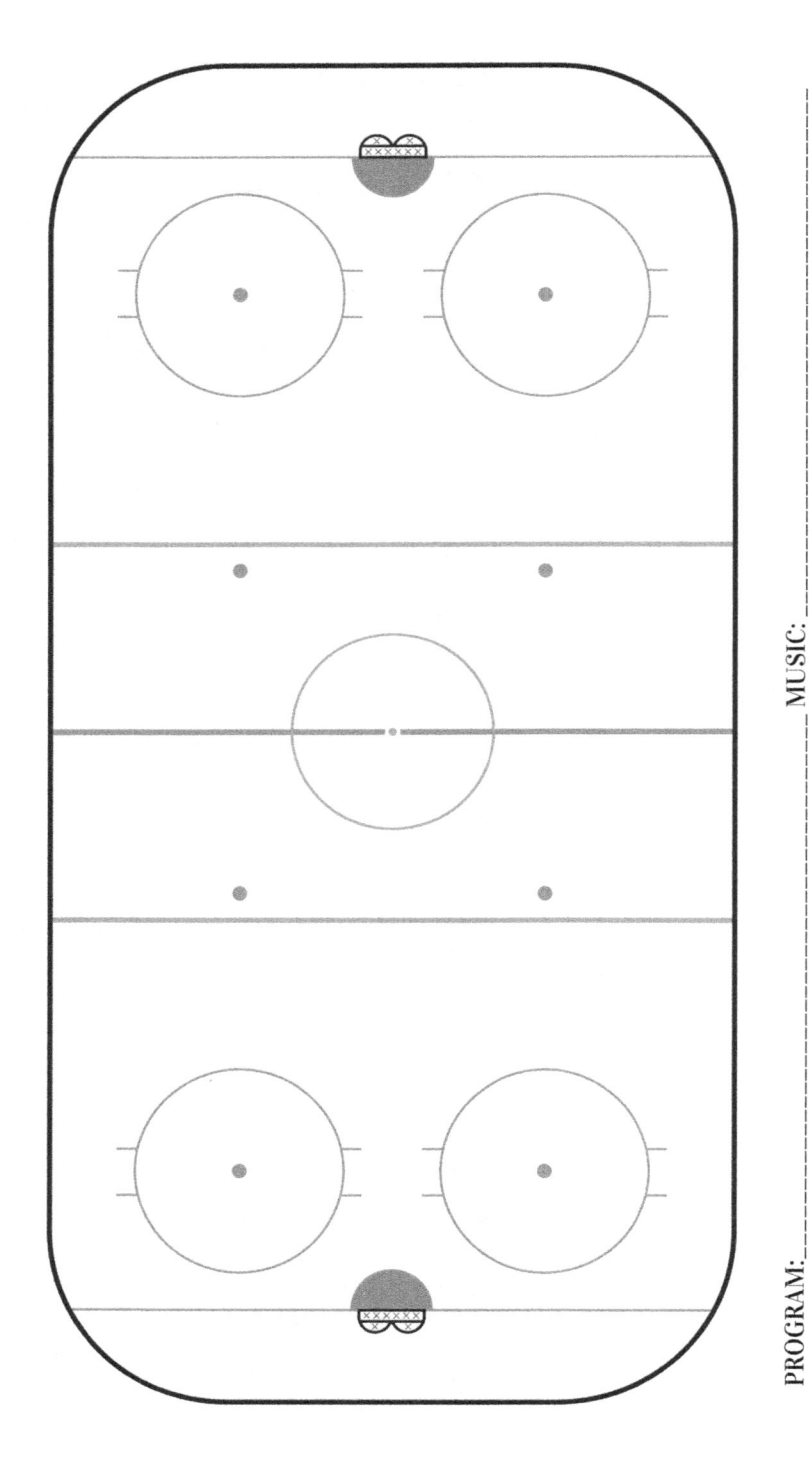

MUSIC: _____

PROGRAM: _____

MY PROGRAM ELEMENTS

PROGRAM_____

MUSIC_____

NOTES

PROGRAM COREOGRAPHY

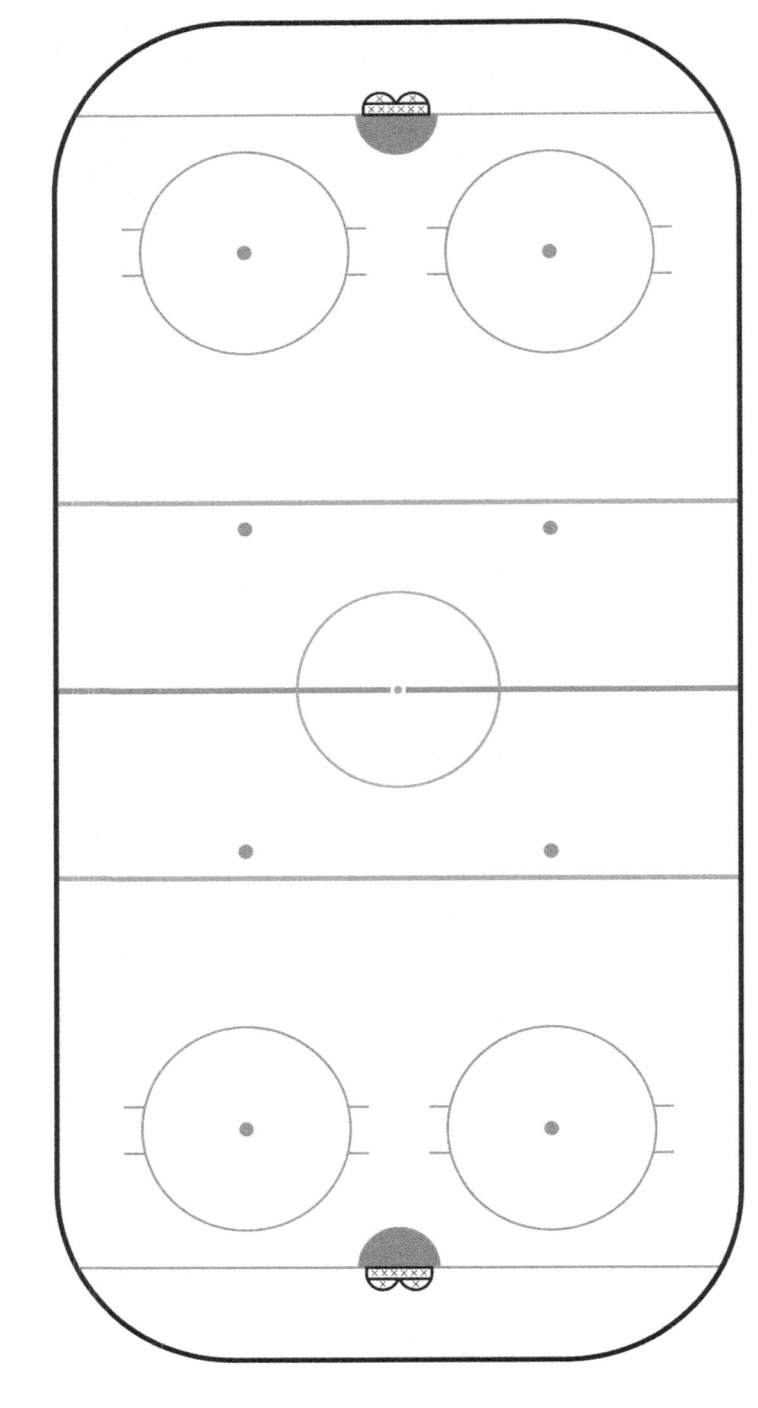

MUSIC: _____

PROGRAM: _____

CONSISTENCY DRILLS

List the elements in your program or that you are working and do five run throughs. Have your coach rate each element and provide feedback.

DATE:

ELEMENT:	1	2	3	4	5	NOTES

MOST IMPROVED ELEMENT:

PROGRAM RUN THRU

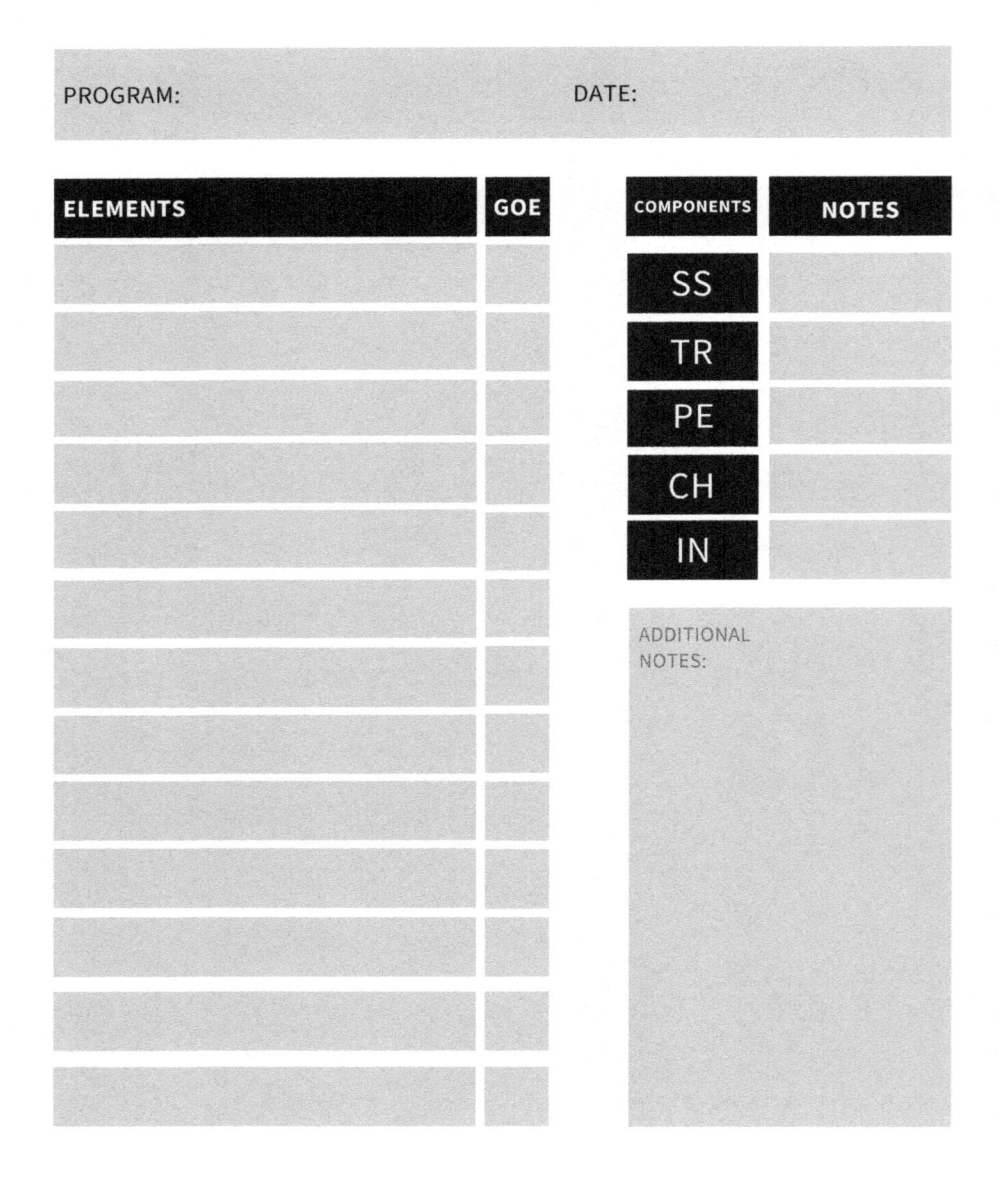

PROGRAM: **DATE:**

ELEMENTS	GOE

COMPONENTS	NOTES
SS	
TR	
PE	
CH	
IN	

ADDITIONAL NOTES:

CONSISTENCY DRILLS

List the elements in your program or that you are working and do five run throughs.
Have your coach rate each element and provide feedback.

DATE:

ELEMENT:	1	2	3	4	5	NOTES

MOST IMPROVED ELEMENT:

PROGRAM RUN THRU

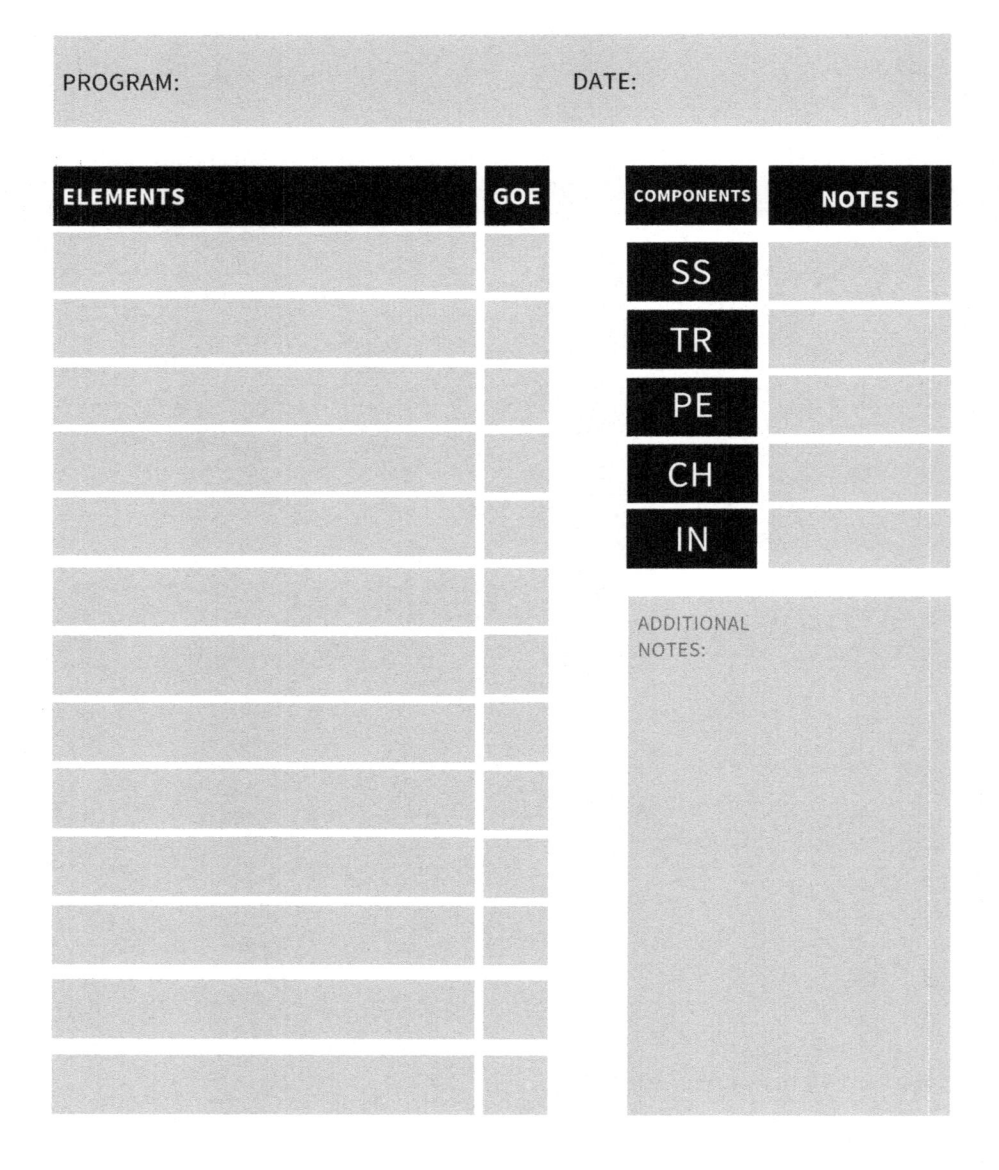

PROGRAM:　　　　　　　　　　DATE:

ELEMENTS	GOE

COMPONENTS	NOTES
SS	
TR	
PE	
CH	
IN	

ADDITIONAL NOTES:

CONSISTENCY DRILLS

List the elements in your program or that you are working and do five run throughs. Have your coach rate each element and provide feedback.

DATE:

ELEMENT:	1	2	3	4	5	NOTES

MOST IMPROVED ELEMENT:

PROGRAM RUN THRU

PROGRAM: **DATE:**

ELEMENTS	GOE

COMPONENTS	NOTES
SS	
TR	
PE	
CH	
IN	

ADDITIONAL NOTES:

CONSISTENCY DRILLS

List the elements in your program or that you are working and do five run throughs. Have your coach rate each element and provide feedback.

DATE:

ELEMENT:	1	2	3	4	5	NOTES

MOST IMPROVED ELEMENT:

PROGRAM RUN THRU

PROGRAM: DATE:

ELEMENTS	GOE

COMPONENTS	NOTES
SS	
TR	
PE	
CH	
IN	

ADDITIONAL NOTES:

CONSISTENCY DRILLS

List the elements in your program or that you are working and do five run throughs. Have your coach rate each element and provide feedback.

DATE:

ELEMENT:	1	2	3	4	5	NOTES

MOST IMPROVED ELEMENT:

PROGRAM RUN THRU

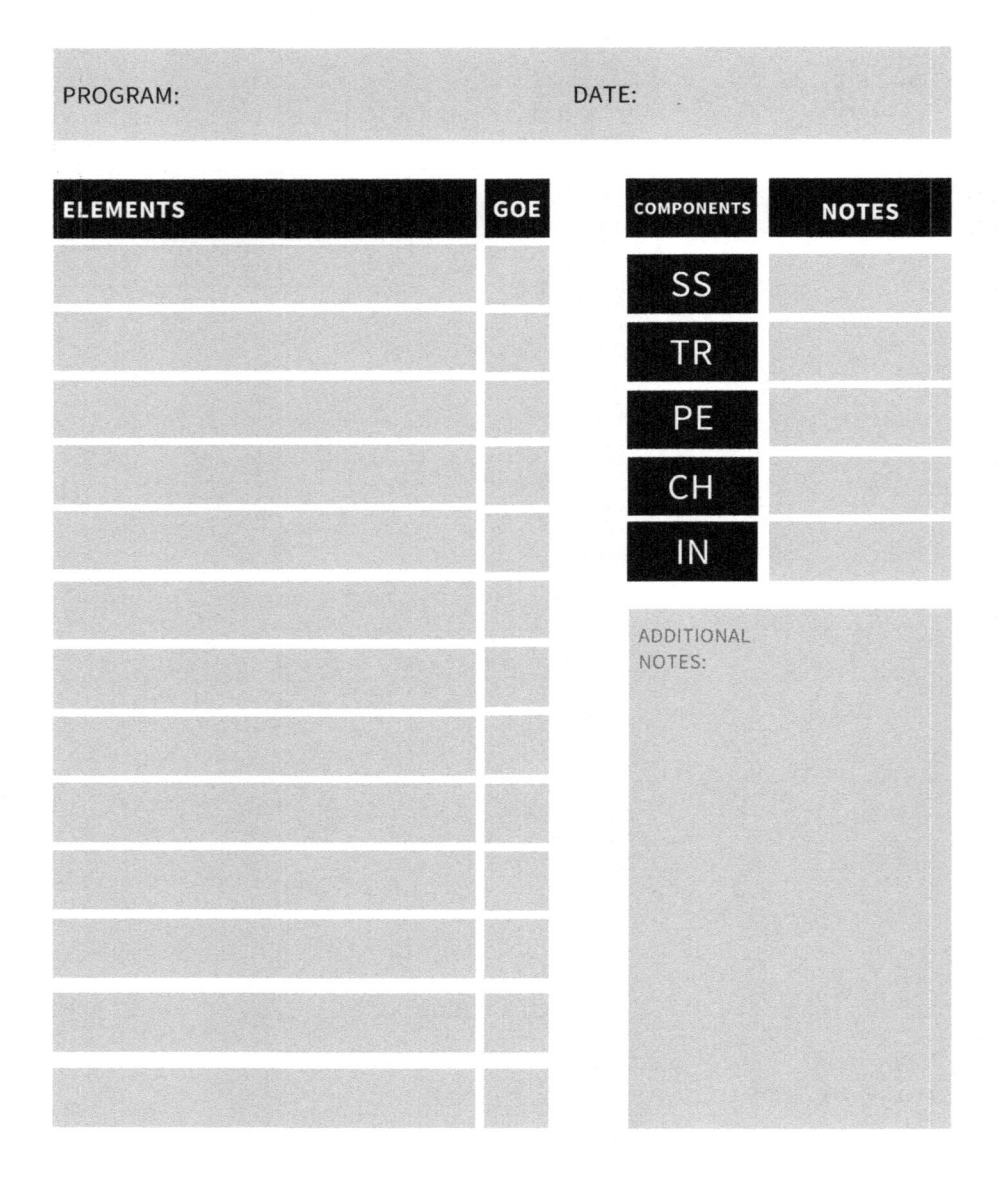

PROGRAM: DATE:

ELEMENTS	GOE

COMPONENTS	NOTES
SS	
TR	
PE	
CH	
IN	

ADDITIONAL NOTES:

CONSISTENCY DRILLS

List the elements in your program or that you are working and do five run throughs. Have your coach rate each element and provide feedback.

DATE:

ELEMENT:	1	2	3	4	5	NOTES

MOST IMPROVED ELEMENT:

PROGRAM RUN THRU

PROGRAM: DATE:

ELEMENTS	GOE

COMPONENTS	NOTES
SS	
TR	
PE	
CH	
IN	

ADDITIONAL NOTES:

CONSISTENCY DRILLS

List the elements in your program or that you are working and do five run throughs. Have your coach rate each element and provide feedback.

DATE:

ELEMENT:	1	2	3	4	5	NOTES

MOST IMPROVED ELEMENT:

PROGRAM RUN THRU

PROGRAM: **DATE:**

ELEMENTS	GOE

COMPONENTS	NOTES
SS	
TR	
PE	
CH	
IN	

ADDITIONAL NOTES:

CONSISTENCY DRILLS

List the elements in your program or that you are working and do five run throughs. Have your coach rate each element and provide feedback.

DATE:

ELEMENT:	1	2	3	4	5	NOTES

MOST IMPROVED ELEMENT:

PROGRAM RUN THRU

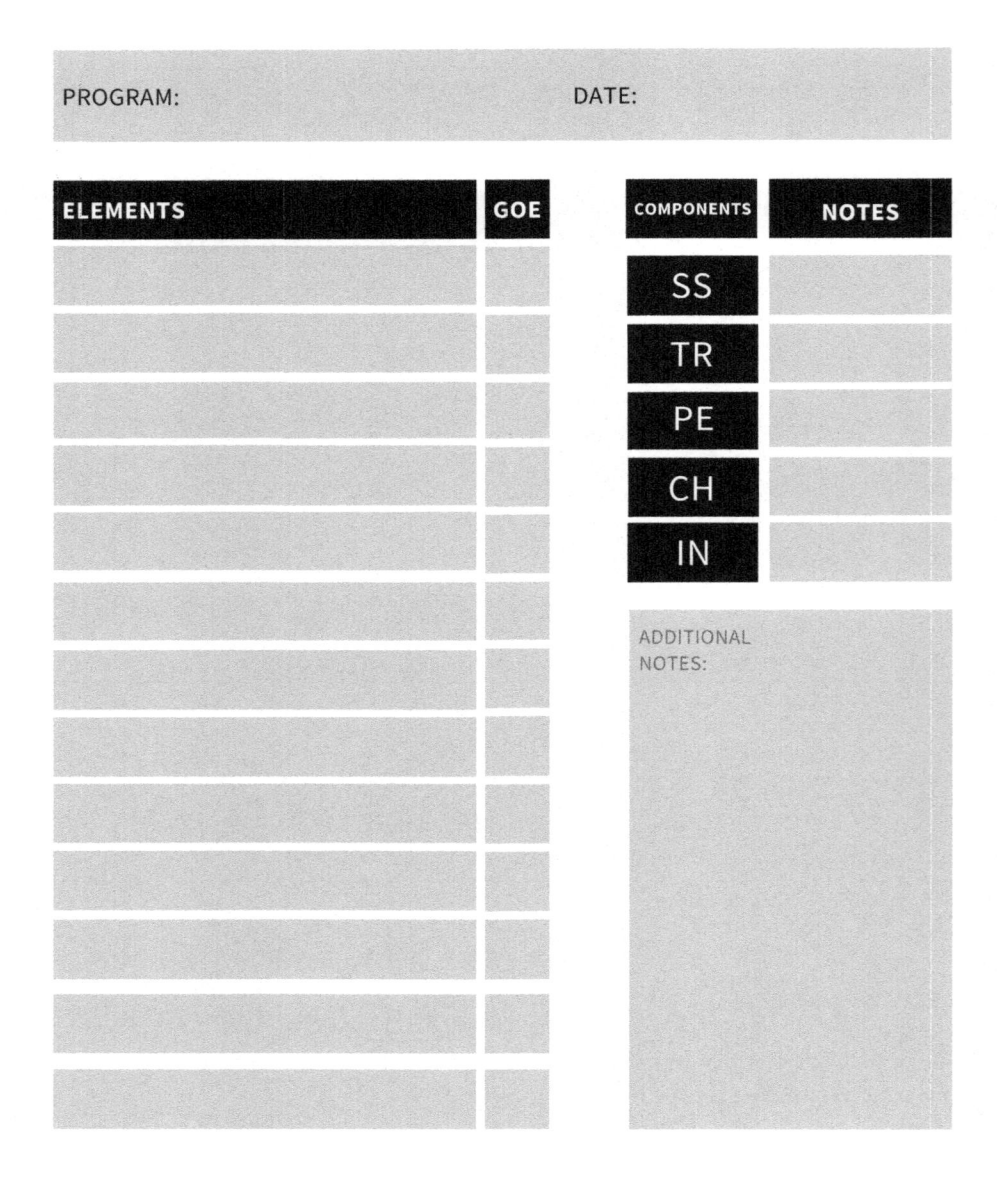

PROGRAM: **DATE:**

ELEMENTS	GOE

COMPONENTS	NOTES
SS	
TR	
PE	
CH	
IN	

ADDITIONAL NOTES:

CONSISTENCY DRILLS

List the elements in your program or that you are working and do five run throughs. Have your coach rate each element and provide feedback.

DATE:

ELEMENT:	1	2	3	4	5	NOTES

MOST IMPROVED ELEMENT:

PROGRAM RUN THRU

PROGRAM: **DATE:**

ELEMENTS	GOE

COMPONENTS	NOTES
SS	
TR	
PE	
CH	
IN	

ADDITIONAL NOTES:

CONSISTENCY DRILLS

List the elements in your program or that you are working and do five run throughs. Have your coach rate each element and provide feedback.

DATE:

ELEMENT:	1	2	3	4	5	NOTES

MOST IMPROVED ELEMENT:

PROGRAM RUN THRU

PROGRAM: **DATE:**

ELEMENTS	GOE

COMPONENTS	NOTES
SS	
TR	
PE	
CH	
IN	

ADDITIONAL NOTES:

CONSISTENCY DRILLS

List the elements in your program or that you are working and do five run throughs. Have your coach rate each element and provide feedback.

DATE:

ELEMENT:	1	2	3	4	5	NOTES

MOST IMPROVED ELEMENT:

PROGRAM RUN THRU

PROGRAM: DATE:

ELEMENTS	GOE

COMPONENTS	NOTES
SS	
TR	
PE	
CH	
IN	

ADDITIONAL NOTES:

CONSISTENCY DRILLS

List the elements in your program or that you are working and do five run throughs. Have your coach rate each element and provide feedback.

DATE:

ELEMENT:	1	2	3	4	5	NOTES

MOST IMPROVED ELEMENT:

PROGRAM RUN THRU

PROGRAM: **DATE:**

ELEMENTS	GOE

COMPONENTS	NOTES
SS	
TR	
PE	
CH	
IN	

ADDITIONAL NOTES:

COMPETITION PLANNING

DATE	LOCATION	EVENTS / LEVEL

MY GOALS FOR THIS COMPETITION:

HOW CAN I MAKE SURE ALL ELEMENTS ARE COUNTED & RECEIVE POSITIVE SCORES?

IS THIS REALISTIC?

HOW WILL I KNOW THAT I HAVE ACHIEVED MY GOALS?

NOTES

COMPETITION PLANNING

DATE	LOCATION	EVENTS / LEVEL

MY GOALS FOR THIS COMPETITION:

HOW CAN I MAKE SURE ALL ELEMENTS ARE COUNTED & RECEIVE POSITIVE SCORES?

IS THIS REALISTIC?

HOW WILL I KNOW THAT I HAVE ACHIEVED MY GOALS?

NOTES

COMPETITION PLANNING

DATE	LOCATION	EVENTS / LEVEL

MY GOALS FOR THIS COMPETITION:

HOW CAN I MAKE SURE ALL ELEMENTS ARE COUNTED & RECEIVE POSITIVE SCORES?

IS THIS REALISTIC?

HOW WILL I KNOW THAT I HAVE ACHIEVED MY GOALS?

NOTES

COMPETITION PLANNING

DATE	LOCATION	EVENTS / LEVEL

MY GOALS FOR THIS COMPETITION:

HOW CAN I MAKE SURE ALL ELEMENTS ARE COUNTED & RECEIVE POSITIVE SCORES?

IS THIS REALISTIC?

HOW WILL I KNOW THAT I HAVE ACHIEVED MY GOALS?

NOTES

COMPETITION PLANNING

DATE	LOCATION	EVENTS / LEVEL

MY GOALS FOR THIS COMPETITION:

HOW CAN I MAKE SURE ALL ELEMENTS ARE COUNTED & RECEIVE POSITIVE SCORES?

IS THIS REALISTIC?

HOW WILL I KNOW THAT I HAVE ACHIEVED MY GOALS?

NOTES

COMPETITION PLANNING

DATE	LOCATION	EVENTS / LEVEL

MY GOALS FOR THIS COMPETITION:

HOW CAN I MAKE SURE ALL ELEMENTS ARE COUNTED & RECEIVE POSITIVE SCORES?

IS THIS REALISTIC?

HOW WILL I KNOW THAT I HAVE ACHIEVED MY GOALS?

NOTES

COMPETITION PLANNING

DATE	LOCATION	EVENTS / LEVEL

MY GOALS FOR THIS COMPETITION:

HOW CAN I MAKE SURE ALL ELEMENTS ARE COUNTED & RECEIVE POSITIVE SCORES?

IS THIS REALISTIC?

HOW WILL I KNOW THAT I HAVE ACHIEVED MY GOALS?

NOTES

COMPETITION PLANNING

DATE	LOCATION	EVENTS / LEVEL

MY GOALS FOR THIS COMPETITION:

HOW CAN I MAKE SURE ALL ELEMENTS ARE COUNTED & RECEIVE POSITIVE SCORES?

IS THIS REALISTIC?

HOW WILL I KNOW THAT I HAVE ACHIEVED MY GOALS?

NOTES

COMPETITION PLANNING

DATE	LOCATION	EVENTS / LEVEL

MY GOALS FOR THIS COMPETITION:

HOW CAN I MAKE SURE ALL ELEMENTS ARE COUNTED & RECEIVE POSITIVE SCORES?

IS THIS REALISTIC?

HOW WILL I KNOW THAT I HAVE ACHIEVED MY GOALS?

NOTES

COMPETITION PLANNING

DATE	LOCATION	EVENTS / LEVEL

MY GOALS FOR THIS COMPETITION:

HOW CAN I MAKE SURE ALL ELEMENTS ARE COUNTED & RECEIVE POSITIVE SCORES?

IS THIS REALISTIC?

HOW WILL I KNOW THAT I HAVE ACHIEVED MY GOALS?

NOTES

COMPETITION PLANNING

DATE	LOCATION	EVENTS / LEVEL

MY GOALS FOR THIS COMPETITION:

HOW CAN I MAKE SURE ALL ELEMENTS ARE COUNTED & RECEIVE POSITIVE SCORES?

IS THIS REALISTIC?

HOW WILL I KNOW THAT I HAVE ACHIEVED MY GOALS?

NOTES

COMPETITION PLANNING

DATE	LOCATION	EVENTS / LEVEL

MY GOALS FOR THIS COMPETITION:

HOW CAN I MAKE SURE ALL ELEMENTS ARE COUNTED & RECEIVE POSITIVE SCORES?

IS THIS REALISTIC?

HOW WILL I KNOW THAT I HAVE ACHIEVED MY GOALS?

NOTES

COMPETITION & TEST
CHECKLIST

YOUR MUSIC

Even if you have uploaded your music, be sure to bring two extra copies on CD (and your phone as a third backup).

HAIR

- Hair spray
- Clips, nets, ties
- Brush
- Accessories
- Mirror

WARDROBE

- Dress/skating outfit
- Undergarmets + back-up
- Tights
- Back-up dress/outfit
- Back-up tights
- Gloves
- Warm-up Jacket

MAKE-UP

- Primer/foundation/powder
- Concealer
- Blush
- Eye shadow, eye liner, mascara, brow definer
- Lip color
- Setting spray
- Make-up remover

EQUIPMENT

- Skates (both of them!)
- Blade guards
- Soakers
- Spare laces
- Padding gel/wraps
- Sneakers, yoga mat, foam roller

JUST IN CASE

- Membership Card
- Screwdriver
- Skate polish
- Nail polish (for runs)
- First Aid kit with bandages
- Needle and thread
- Femine hygiene products
- Tissues
- Phone and charger

COMPETITION RESULTS

DATE	LOCATION	EVENTS / LEVEL

MY PROGRAM SCORES AND PLACEMENTS:

ANY PERSONAL BESTS?

WHAT DID I DO WELL?
1.

2.

3.

WHAT CAN I DO DIFFERENTLY NEXT TIME?
1.

2.

3.

COACH'S NOTES

COMPETITION RESULTS

DATE	LOCATION	EVENTS / LEVEL

MY PROGRAM SCORES AND PLACEMENTS:

ANY PERSONAL BESTS?

WHAT DID I DO WELL?
1.

2.

3.

WHAT CAN I DO DIFFERENTLY NEXT TIME?
1.

2.

3.

COACH'S NOTES

COMPETITION RESULTS

DATE	LOCATION	EVENTS / LEVEL

MY PROGRAM SCORES AND PLACEMENTS:

ANY PERSONAL BESTS?

WHAT DID I DO WELL?
1.

2.

3.

WHAT CAN I DO DIFFERENTLY NEXT TIME?
1.

2.

3.

COACH'S NOTES

COMPETITION RESULTS

DATE	LOCATION	EVENTS / LEVEL

MY PROGRAM SCORES AND PLACEMENTS:

ANY PERSONAL BESTS?

WHAT DID I DO WELL?
1.

2.

3.

WHAT CAN I DO DIFFERENTLY NEXT TIME?
1.

2.

3.

COACH'S NOTES

COMPETITION RESULTS

DATE	LOCATION	EVENTS / LEVEL

MY PROGRAM SCORES AND PLACEMENTS:

ANY PERSONAL BESTS?

WHAT DID I DO WELL?
1.

2.

3.

WHAT CAN I DO DIFFERENTLY NEXT TIME?
1.

2.

3.

COACH'S NOTES

COMPETITION RESULTS

DATE	LOCATION	EVENTS / LEVEL

MY PROGRAM SCORES AND PLACEMENTS:

ANY PERSONAL BESTS?

WHAT DID I DO WELL?
1.

2.

3.

WHAT CAN I DO DIFFERENTLY NEXT TIME?
1.

2.

3.

COACH'S NOTES

COMPETITION RESULTS

DATE	LOCATION	EVENTS / LEVEL

MY PROGRAM SCORES AND PLACEMENTS:

ANY PERSONAL BESTS?

WHAT DID I DO WELL?
1.

2.

3.

WHAT CAN I DO DIFFERENTLY NEXT TIME?
1.

2.

3.

COACH'S NOTES

COMPETITION RESULTS

DATE	LOCATION	EVENTS / LEVEL

MY PROGRAM SCORES AND PLACEMENTS:

ANY PERSONAL BESTS?

WHAT DID I DO WELL?
1.

2.

3.

WHAT CAN I DO DIFFERENTLY NEXT TIME?
1.

2.

3.

COACH'S NOTES

COMPETITION RESULTS

DATE	LOCATION	EVENTS / LEVEL

MY PROGRAM SCORES AND PLACEMENTS:

ANY PERSONAL BESTS?

WHAT DID I DO WELL?
1.

2.

3.

WHAT CAN I DO DIFFERENTLY NEXT TIME?
1.

2.

3.

COACH'S NOTES

COMPETITION RESULTS

DATE	LOCATION	EVENTS / LEVEL

MY PROGRAM SCORES AND PLACEMENTS:

ANY PERSONAL BESTS?

WHAT DID I DO WELL?
1.

2.

3.

WHAT CAN I DO DIFFERENTLY NEXT TIME?
1.

2.

3.

COACH'S NOTES

COMPETITION RESULTS

DATE	LOCATION	EVENTS / LEVEL

MY PROGRAM SCORES AND PLACEMENTS:

ANY PERSONAL BESTS?

WHAT DID I DO WELL?
1.

2.

3.

WHAT CAN I DO DIFFERENTLY NEXT TIME?
1.

2.

3.

COACH'S NOTES

COMPETITION RESULTS

DATE	LOCATION	EVENTS / LEVEL

MY PROGRAM SCORES AND PLACEMENTS:

ANY PERSONAL BESTS?

WHAT DID I DO WELL?
1.
2.
3.

WHAT CAN I DO DIFFERENTLY NEXT TIME?
1.
2.
3.

COACH'S NOTES

EVALUATE!

MONTH REFLECTION: _ _ _ _ _ _ _ _ _ _ _ _ _ _ _

LAST MONTH IN ONE WORD

HIGHLIGHTS

CHALLENGES

REWARD FOR ACHIEVEMENTS

HOW TO IMPROVE MYSELF?

THOUGHTS

MONTHLY GOALS _____

FOCUS ON

SKATING GOALS
- ○
- ○
- ○
- ○
- ○
- ○
- ○

WHY?

PERSONAL GOALS
- ○
- ○
- ○
- ○
- ○
- ○
- ○

NOTES

EDUCATION/ WORK GOALS
- ○
- ○
- ○
- ○
- ○
- ○
- ○

MY NOTES

COACH'S NOTES

MONTH REFLECTION: _____

LAST MONTH IN ONE WORD

HIGHLIGHTS

CHALLENGES

REWARD FOR ACHIEVEMENTS

HOW TO IMPROVE MYSELF?

THOUGHTS

MONTHLY GOALS _ _ _ _ _ _ _ _ _ _ _ _ _ _ _ _ _ _ _

FOCUS ON

SKATING GOALS
-
-
-
-
-
-
-

WHY?

PERSONAL GOALS
-
-
-
-
-
-
-

NOTES

EDUCATION/ WORK GOALS
-
-
-
-
-
-

MY NOTES

COACH'S NOTES

MONTH REFLECTION: _____

LAST MONTH IN ONE WORD

HIGHLIGHTS

CHALLENGES

REWARD FOR ACHIEVEMENTS

HOW TO IMPROVE MYSELF?

THOUGHTS

MONTHLY GOALS _____

FOCUS ON

SKATING GOALS
-
-
-
-
-
-
-

WHY?

PERSONAL GOALS
-
-
-
-
-
-
-

NOTES

EDUCATION/ WORK GOALS
-
-
-
-
-
-
-

MY NOTES

COACH'S NOTES

MONTH REFLECTION: _____

LAST MONTH IN ONE WORD

HIGHLIGHTS	CHALLENGES

REWARD FOR ACHIEVEMENTS	HOW TO IMPROVE MYSELF?

THOUGHTS

MONTHLY GOALS _____

FOCUS ON

SKATING GOALS
○
○
○
○
○
○
○

WHY?

PERSONAL GOALS
○
○
○
○
○
○
○

NOTES

EDUCATION/ WORK GOALS
○
○
○
○
○
○
○

MY NOTES

COACH'S NOTES

MONTH REFLECTION: _____

LAST MONTH IN ONE WORD

HIGHLIGHTS

CHALLENGES

REWARD FOR ACHIEVEMENTS

HOW TO IMPROVE MYSELF?

THOUGHTS

MONTHLY GOALS _____

FOCUS ON

SKATING GOALS
- ○
- ○
- ○
- ○
- ○
- ○
- ○

WHY?

PERSONAL GOALS
- ○
- ○
- ○
- ○
- ○
- ○
- ○

NOTES

EDUCATION/ WORK GOALS
- ○
- ○
- ○
- ○
- ○
- ○
- ○

MY NOTES

COACH'S NOTES

MONTH REFLECTION: _____

LAST MONTH IN ONE WORD

HIGHLIGHTS

CHALLENGES

REWARD FOR ACHIEVEMENTS

HOW TO IMPROVE MYSELF?

THOUGHTS

MONTHLY GOALS _____

FOCUS ON

SKATING GOALS
-
-
-
-
-
-
-

WHY?

PERSONAL GOALS
-
-
-
-
-
-
-

NOTES

EDUCATION/ WORK GOALS
-
-
-
-
-
-
-

MY NOTES

COACH'S NOTES

MONTH REFLECTION: _____

LAST MONTH IN ONE WORD

HIGHLIGHTS

CHALLENGES

REWARD FOR ACHIEVEMENTS

HOW TO IMPROVE MYSELF?

THOUGHTS

MONTHLY GOALS _ _ _ _ _ _ _ _ _ _ _ _ _ _ _ _ _ _

FOCUS ON

SKATING GOALS
- ○
- ○
- ○
- ○
- ○
- ○
- ○

WHY?

PERSONAL GOALS
- ○
- ○
- ○
- ○
- ○
- ○
- ○

NOTES

EDUCATION/ WORK GOALS
- ○
- ○
- ○
- ○
- ○
- ○
- ○

MY NOTES

COACH'S NOTES

MONTH REFLECTION: _____

LAST MONTH IN ONE WORD

HIGHLIGHTS

CHALLENGES

REWARD FOR ACHIEVEMENTS

HOW TO IMPROVE MYSELF?

THOUGHTS

MONTHLY GOALS _____

FOCUS ON

SKATING GOALS

- ○
- ○
- ○
- ○
- ○
- ○
- ○

WHY?

PERSONAL GOALS

- ○
- ○
- ○
- ○
- ○
- ○
- ○

NOTES

EDUCATION/ WORK GOALS

- ○
- ○
- ○
- ○
- ○
- ○
- ○

MY NOTES

COACH'S NOTES

MONTH REFLECTION: _ _ _ _ _ _ _ _ _ _ _ _ _ _ _

LAST MONTH IN ONE WORD

HIGHLIGHTS

CHALLENGES

REWARD FOR ACHIEVEMENTS

HOW TO IMPROVE MYSELF?

THOUGHTS

MONTHLY GOALS _____

FOCUS ON

SKATING GOALS

- ○
- ○
- ○
- ○
- ○
- ○
- ○

WHY?

PERSONAL GOALS

- ○
- ○
- ○
- ○
- ○
- ○
- ○

NOTES

EDUCATION/ WORK GOALS

- ○
- ○
- ○
- ○
- ○
- ○
- ○

MY NOTES

COACH'S NOTES

MONTH REFLECTION: _ _ _ _ _ _ _ _ _ _ _ _ _ _

LAST MONTH IN ONE WORD

HIGHLIGHTS

CHALLENGES

REWARD FOR ACHIEVEMENTS

HOW TO IMPROVE MYSELF?

THOUGHTS

MONTHLY GOALS _____

FOCUS ON

SKATING GOALS
- ○
- ○
- ○
- ○
- ○
- ○
- ○

WHY?

PERSONAL GOALS
- ○
- ○
- ○
- ○
- ○
- ○
- ○

NOTES

EDUCATION/ WORK GOALS
- ○
- ○
- ○
- ○
- ○
- ○
- ○

MY NOTES

COACH'S NOTES

MONTH REFLECTION: _____

LAST MONTH IN ONE WORD

HIGHLIGHTS

CHALLENGES

REWARD FOR ACHIEVEMENTS

HOW TO IMPROVE MYSELF?

THOUGHTS

MONTHLY GOALS _____

FOCUS ON

SKATING GOALS
- ○
- ○
- ○
- ○
- ○
- ○
- ○

WHY?

PERSONAL GOALS
- ○
- ○
- ○
- ○
- ○
- ○
- ○

NOTES

EDUCATION/ WORK GOALS
- ○
- ○
- ○
- ○
- ○
- ○
- ○

MY NOTES

COACH'S NOTES

MONTH REFLECTION: _____

LAST MONTH IN ONE WORD

HIGHLIGHTS	CHALLENGES

REWARD FOR ACHIEVEMENTS	HOW TO IMPROVE MYSELF?

THOUGHTS

MONTHLY GOALS _____

FOCUS ON

SKATING GOALS
- ○
- ○
- ○
- ○
- ○
- ○
- ○

WHY?

PERSONAL GOALS
- ○
- ○
- ○
- ○
- ○
- ○
- ○

NOTES

EDUCATION/ WORK GOALS
- ○
- ○
- ○
- ○
- ○
- ○
- ○

MY NOTES

COACH'S NOTES

MONTH REFLECTION: _____

LAST MONTH IN ONE WORD

HIGHLIGHTS	CHALLENGES

REWARD FOR ACHIEVEMENTS

HOW TO IMPROVE MYSELF?

THOUGHTS

MONTHLY GOALS _____

FOCUS ON

SKATING GOALS
- ○
- ○
- ○
- ○
- ○
- ○
- ○

WHY?

PERSONAL GOALS
- ○
- ○
- ○
- ○
- ○
- ○
- ○

NOTES

EDUCATION/ WORK GOALS
- ○
- ○
- ○
- ○
- ○
- ○
- ○

MY NOTES

COACH'S NOTES

PARENT & COACH COMMUNICATION

DATE:
_____
_____
_____
_____

PARENT SIGNATURE:　　　　　　COACH SIGNATURE:

DATE:
_____
_____
_____
_____

PARENT SIGNATURE:　　　　　　COACH SIGNATURE:

DATE:
_____
_____
_____
_____

PARENT SIGNATURE:　　　　　　COACH SIGNATURE:

DATE:
_____
_____
_____
_____

PARENT SIGNATURE:　　　　　　COACH SIGNATURE:

PARENT & COACH COMMUNICATION

DATE: _____

_____
_____
_____

PARENT SIGNATURE: _____ COACH SIGNATURE: _____

DATE: _____

_____
_____
_____

PARENT SIGNATURE: _____ COACH SIGNATURE: _____

DATE: _____

_____
_____
_____

PARENT SIGNATURE: _____ COACH SIGNATURE: _____

DATE: _____

_____
_____
_____

PARENT SIGNATURE: _____ COACH SIGNATURE: _____

PARENT & COACH COMMUNICATION

DATE: _____

_____
_____
_____
_____

PARENT SIGNATURE: _____ COACH SIGNATURE: _____

DATE: _____

_____
_____
_____
_____

PARENT SIGNATURE: _____ COACH SIGNATURE: _____

DATE: _____

_____
_____
_____
_____

PARENT SIGNATURE: _____ COACH SIGNATURE: _____

DATE: _____

_____
_____
_____
_____

PARENT SIGNATURE: _____ COACH SIGNATURE: _____

PARENT & COACH COMMUNICATION

DATE: _____
_____
_____
_____
_____

PARENT SIGNATURE: _____   COACH SIGNATURE: _____

DATE: _____
_____
_____
_____
_____

PARENT SIGNATURE: _____   COACH SIGNATURE: _____

DATE: _____
_____
_____
_____
_____

PARENT SIGNATURE: _____   COACH SIGNATURE: _____

DATE: _____
_____
_____
_____
_____

PARENT SIGNATURE: _____   COACH SIGNATURE: _____

PARENT & COACH COMMUNICATION

DATE: _____
_____
_____
_____

PARENT SIGNATURE: _____ COACH SIGNATURE: _____

DATE: _____
_____
_____
_____

PARENT SIGNATURE: _____ COACH SIGNATURE: _____

DATE: _____
_____
_____
_____

PARENT SIGNATURE: _____ COACH SIGNATURE: _____

DATE: _____
_____
_____
_____

PARENT SIGNATURE: _____ COACH SIGNATURE: _____

PARENT & COACH COMMUNICATION

DATE:
_____
_____
_____
_____

PARENT SIGNATURE: _____ COACH SIGNATURE: _____

DATE:
_____
_____
_____
_____

PARENT SIGNATURE: _____ COACH SIGNATURE: _____

DATE:
_____
_____
_____
_____

PARENT SIGNATURE: _____ COACH SIGNATURE: _____

DATE:
_____
_____
_____
_____

PARENT SIGNATURE: _____ COACH SIGNATURE: _____

PARENT & COACH COMMUNICATION

DATE: _____
_____
_____
_____
_____

PARENT SIGNATURE: _____ COACH SIGNATURE: _____

DATE: _____
_____
_____
_____
_____

PARENT SIGNATURE: _____ COACH SIGNATURE: _____

DATE: _____
_____
_____
_____
_____

PARENT SIGNATURE: _____ COACH SIGNATURE: _____

DATE: _____
_____
_____
_____
_____

PARENT SIGNATURE: _____ COACH SIGNATURE: _____

PARENT & COACH COMMUNICATION

DATE: _____

_____
_____
_____
_____

PARENT SIGNATURE: _____   COACH SIGNATURE: _____

DATE: _____

_____
_____
_____
_____

PARENT SIGNATURE: _____   COACH SIGNATURE: _____

DATE: _____

_____
_____
_____
_____

PARENT SIGNATURE: _____   COACH SIGNATURE: _____

DATE: _____

_____
_____
_____
_____

PARENT SIGNATURE: _____   COACH SIGNATURE: _____

PARENT & COACH COMMUNICATION

DATE: _____
_____
_____
_____
_____

PARENT SIGNATURE: _____ COACH SIGNATURE: _____

DATE: _____
_____
_____
_____
_____

PARENT SIGNATURE: _____ COACH SIGNATURE: _____

DATE: _____
_____
_____
_____
_____

PARENT SIGNATURE: _____ COACH SIGNATURE: _____

DATE: _____
_____
_____
_____
_____

PARENT SIGNATURE: _____ COACH SIGNATURE: _____

PARENT & COACH COMMUNICATION

DATE: _____
_____
_____
_____
_____

PARENT SIGNATURE: _____ COACH SIGNATURE: _____

DATE: _____
_____
_____
_____
_____

PARENT SIGNATURE: _____ COACH SIGNATURE: _____

DATE: _____
_____
_____
_____
_____

PARENT SIGNATURE: _____ COACH SIGNATURE: _____

DATE: _____
_____
_____
_____
_____

PARENT SIGNATURE: _____ COACH SIGNATURE: _____

PARENT & COACH COMMUNICATION

DATE: _____

_____
_____
_____
_____

PARENT SIGNATURE: _____   COACH SIGNATURE: _____

DATE: _____

_____
_____
_____
_____

PARENT SIGNATURE: _____   COACH SIGNATURE: _____

DATE: _____

_____
_____
_____
_____

PARENT SIGNATURE: _____   COACH SIGNATURE: _____

DATE: _____

_____
_____
_____
_____

PARENT SIGNATURE: _____   COACH SIGNATURE: _____

PARENT & COACH COMMUNICATION

DATE:
_____
_____
_____
_____

PARENT SIGNATURE: COACH SIGNATURE:

DATE:
_____
_____
_____
_____

PARENT SIGNATURE: COACH SIGNATURE:

DATE:
_____
_____
_____
_____

PARENT SIGNATURE: COACH SIGNATURE:

DATE:
_____
_____
_____
_____

PARENT SIGNATURE: COACH SIGNATURE:

Made in the USA
Las Vegas, NV
16 March 2023